THE STORY OF SEVENOAKS MARKET

THE STORY OF SEVENOAKS MARKET

Published by

KEMSING HERITAGE CENTRE

www.kemsingheritagecentre.org.uk

Chairman: Erica Cole MBE, 5a, Park Lane Kemsing
Kent TN15 6NU

Copyright © A. M. PARKIN 2009

ISBN13   978 – 1 – 87125 – 06 – 9

Photography input : Ron Harding   Jane Bowden

Design : Janet Jones

Additional photography: A.M. Parkin

Illustrations: Map of Domesday Manors H.W. Knocker. **Artwork**: *page 3* B. Fenner; *page 14* R. Edwards; *page 18* C. Essenhigh Corke; *page 25* C. Essenhigh Corke; *page 27* L. Cole; *page 31* C. Essenhigh Corke; *page 41* A.M. Parkin.

Other illustrations gathered from such a wide range of sources in books and library collections for slides made in 1999 / 2000 that it is impossible now to credit them.

Cover illustrations : Livestock market, High Street, 1860s; Livestock market, 1999 Saturday market, 2009; Wednesday market, 2009.

PREFACE

In August, 1999, Sevenoaks livestock market closed. For a few weeks before its closure, I went along each Monday to take photographs of what seemed a colourful subject as well as something of historical interest. At that point I had no intention of giving talks or writing about the market.

But Gordon Day of Pattullo & Partners, who ran the market, asked if I would show my slides at the annual Fat Stock Association dinner that autumn. I agreed, but felt I ought to say a little about the market's history, and so the talk 'The Story of Sevenoaks Market' was born.

After more research, I gave the talk to various historical societies and to Kent Archaeological Society. It is this talk that Erica Cole of Kemsing Heritage Centre has asked me to write up as part of their publishing programme.

As with the talk, I have far more material than I can include without clouding the narrative, but this is the basic story of Sevenoaks market as I read it – bearing in mind we are all open to correction.

Monty Parkin, 2009

The local manors at Domesday, 1086. The manor of Otford stretched from Shoreham to Penshurst. Sevenoaks was an insignificant part.

THE STORY OF SEVENOAKS MARKET

Today there are three small markets held each week in Sevenoaks. On Saturdays, a greengrocer, a flower seller and a few other traders set up stalls beside the High Street by The Chequers Inn. This market is of ancient origin and is a survivor from the medieval market held in the High Street since the 13th century.

A short way northwards, at the new Bligh's development, green and white striped stalls selling mainly jewellery and craft take part in the Bligh's Craft and Country Market. This is of very recent origin.

On Wednesdays, a general market is held in the car park beside the bus station. This is what remains of the huge general market begun at the site next to Sevenoaks station in the 1960s. The Sevenoaks station site, where the tasteful office building now stands, is also where the livestock market was held until 1999.

The two markets with a real history are the Saturday one by The Chequers and the now defunct livestock market. They can both be traced back to the 1280s in the High Street and even earlier to a site by St. Nicholas church because, in Sevenoaks, the origin of the market goes back to the origin of the town itself. In fact local historian Herbert Knocker suggested the market preceded the church and the manor.

Sevenoaks itself was originally a minor, and indeed poor part of the Archbishop of Canterbury's huge manor of Otford.

When Otford was already established in the early 10th century, Sevenoaks was still a 'gorse-grown waste'. The name 'Sevenoaks' is a nature name meaning exactly what it says.

The manor of Otford stretched from Shoreham in the north to Penshurst in the south. It is assumed that a market existed in Otford in Anglo-Saxon times but there is no actual record of one.

Sevenoaks developed on the drove road from Otford going south because each year, in late summer, pigs were driven down into the Wealden forest to feed on the acorns and beech mast. (Weald – *wald* = 'forest'; *hurst* = 'wood').

Pigs were driven south from Otford into the forest to feed on acorns and beech mast.

Feeding pigs in the forest was common in all Kentish manors and, gradually, clearings in the forest developed known as 'dens' (*den baera-*'swine pastures') and this explains all those Wealden names ending in *'den'* – Tenterden, Biddenden, Rolvenden and, more locally, Hollanden. There are over 500 den names in Kent.

The Lord of the Manor, the Archbishop, made a charge for the right to pasture pigs in his forest. It is interesting to note that early records show outsiders [*forinsecorum*) were charged twice as much for this privilege as the lord's own tenants. As we'll see, when the market developed, there seems to have been a local bias here too, giving local people first option when buying and selling in the market place.

The drove road from Otford eventually linked up with other tracks in the Weald to become a very important road, the London to the coast road, connecting London with Rye, Winchelsea and Hastings. The modern equivalent would be the A21.

So, joining the swineherds from the 10th century onwards were merchants from the coast dealing in salt, ironware, imported goods and later, fish.

It is thought early travellers set up a roadside chapel dedicated to St. Nicholas and trading began here.

Perhaps these merchants first set up a chapel by the roadside dedicated to St. Nicholas, the patron saint of travellers, merchants and sailors, and then a market developed beside the church because, in Saxon times, markets were commonly held in churchyards. Or it could have been the other way round and trading began before a chapel was erected. Whichever came first, St. Nicholas developed as both a church and a market place.

The attraction of trading in this out of the way area would have been freedom from controls and tolls imposed by the Lord of the Manor. It would have been a so-called 'boundary market', springing up spontaneously because of its position on the road coming up from the coast and close to another ancient route to the west via Oak Lane.

Of course we have no documentary evidence for this. Domesday Book (1086) shows eleven markets in Kent. Rochester and Canterbury would have had Roman markets and both are credited with very early Saxon fairs and markets (7th century). Other Domesday markets are mainly coastal, like Dover. Sevenoaks is not listed as a settlement or a market, it was a subordinate part of Otford, but if it had a free market, of no value to the Lord of the Manor, there would have been no need to include it in the manorial account as Domesday is only concerned with value.

Most markets in Kent began later with a founding charter, set up as a money-making exercise for a royal favourite, charging tolls, but no founding charter has been found for Sevenoaks, suggesting it is a pre-Conquest, toll free market, held by ancient custom. All later official references to Sevenoaks simply confirm existing rights. When a Royal Commission discussed Sevenoaks market in the 1880s it was stated that Sevenoaks market had existed since 'time immemorial'. It seems clear that Herbert Knocker and others are right in believing the origin of the market is closely connected with the origin of the town itself.

An important trade which grew up along the coast road was the fish trade from Rye. Records show this trade as being important to Rye from at least the 1140s. The men of Rye had an ancient privilege to supply the king's court with fish.

The main catch was herring, some of which might be shipped to London in barrels. But also, along with cod, mackerel and other fish, it was transported from Rye on trains of pack horses coming up the old drove road. The fish was carried in wicker baskets slung over the horses. The Old Norse name for a wicker basket was *'hrip'*, and the men from Rye in charge of the pack horses were known as 'rippiers'.

Because sea fish do not survive long once caught, even if kept damp in straw, transport had to be quick and, surprisingly, it was reckoned that fish landed very early in the morning at Rye could reach London the same day.

Although much of the fish from Rye was destined for London via Chipstead, where there was an easy crossing of the river Darent, no doubt some of the fish was off-loaded at Sevenoaks. The route of the Rye road coming from Tonbridge via Riverhill had several variations, including a route via Whitley Mill to Sevenoaks, passing the exact spot in the High Street where the small Saturday market is still held to this day.

Because of the fish trade, another market developed at Chipstead and Bessels Green. The name Chipstead means 'market place'. It comes from the old English *'ceap'*, to trade, *'ceapian'*, to buy. From this we get Chipping Norton, Chipping Campden, Cheapside, Chepstow,

Chipstead, all of which mean 'market place'. The word chapman means 'dealer'.

Chipstead is first mentioned in 1191 and it's likely fish from Rye was being traded there at this early date. London fishmongers, as well as the Royal Purveyor, came to buy fish at Chipstead market. In nearby fields, a local metal detectorist has found many small denomination coins, usually a sign of a market place. These date from as early as Henry III (1216 – 1272).

Fish traders from Rye came to the market at Chipstead. Fish were salted for preservation at Salters Heath.

The fish was delivered as fresh as possible, but if necessary it could be preserved by salting at Salters Heath. Other reminders of the fish trade here are Mackerels Plain, Cods Field (Brittains Lane) and Cods Corner Wood (Croft Way), all a legacy of the fish trade from Rye.

The Rye fish trade declined towards the end of the 16th century when Rye harbour was silting up. Rye then became a minor market town and the great days of the rippiers carrying fish up the Rye road to the markets at Chipstead and Sevenoaks were over.

The market moved from the churchyard to this wide area of road opposite Sevenoaks School. Oak Lane was an ancient route westwards.

But Sevenoaks market, handling a much wider range of goods, continued to flourish and expanded out of the churchyard to the area by Oak Lane and the Old Post Office, where the road widens opposite Sevenoaks School. Such a wide stretch of road is an indicator of an early market place.

This move could have been a natural one or it might have been prompted by royal orders against holding markets in churchyards. But this was a good position for trade, on the old drove road, now the coast road to the south, and at the junction with Oak Lane which brought traffic from the west. There is evidence for very early traffic and trade east / west along the Holmesdale Valley, from the Bronze Age onwards.

The Old Post Office (centre), an early 15th century building on an earlier site, expanded backwards and probably had a shop at the front. It is set at an interesting angle to the road, as though it could have been beside a market triangle. Medieval markets were often triangular. Below the road surface close to the Old Post Office are cobbles.

Apart from the physical evidence, and a little archaeological evidence in the form of coin finds, there is no documentary record of the market here, but this clearly was a market area.

From the 1280s, records show the market here, where the road divides. In the centre was the market triangle. The later building on the left was the reeve's house. He collected rents from the shops for the Lord of the Manor.

At some point in the 13th century the market moved further up the road to another favourable junction, the point where the Riverhead/London road separates from the Otford/Maidstone one by the present day fountain. We know this because the first documentary references to the market in the 1280s place it here and in fact imply the market had been held at this spot for some time.

The market developed here into one of the great markets of Kent. In the centre was the market triangle where stalls were set up. These would have gradually evolved into booths and then shops. As mentioned, medieval markets were often triangular, this being considered a good shape to give every trader a fair chance. Whether by accident or design, the modern Bluewater shopping centre is triangular.

The market day was Saturday. As well as the market stalls, animals – cattle, sheep, pigs – would have filled the High Street. The wide paved area between The Chequers Inn and Lloyds TSB bank is still known as the market square, a square within a triangle, and this is where those few stalls still trade each Saturday, maintaining a link with the medieval market. Once, one of the present day traders, on being booked by a traffic warden, quoted Magna Carta in his defence and claimed, rightly, that market traders had been here long before traffic wardens and yellow lines.

On the left is the 15th century building, currently Loch Fyne restaurant, which is thought to be the reeve's house, the office and home of the archbishop's agent who collected rents from the shops in the nearby market place.

The central passageway through the market triangle.

Running north/south through the centre of the market triangle today is still a central passageway. The stalls, seven feet by two feet, were originally laid out on a grid system with other alleyways crossing the central one at right angles.

Stallholders would sometimes leave their stalls in place from one market to another to create permanent structures. These would become liable for rent. Buildings developed backwards from a narrow selling area at the front where a stall once stood.

This area, The Shambles, was where meat and fish were sold. During a recent conversion of the office building, now Cavendish estate agents, under the floor the builder found masses of shells from shellfish, a sign of its earlier use as a fishmonger's. Many buildings here have substantial cellars originally built for storage of market goods. One shop (opposite No. 2, The Shambles) has an interesting mullioned window and a handsome crown post roof.

So the stalls turned into shops and, by the late 13th century, shops paying rent to the Archbishop of Canterbury are mentioned. But there is no record of market tolls ever being charged.

A busy medieval market with the barber operating in the centre.

The illustration gives a good idea of a medieval market place. However, in Sevenoaks, we know the buildings were not tiled but wooden with thatched roofs, as there are records of the archbishop spending money on their reconstruction, the timber coming from Brittains farm and the thatch from Seal.

Craft surnames gradually become more common in market deeds, indicating a variety of occupations – carpenter, weaver, tailor, saddler, cooper. It is thought that Kent had such lively markets partly because of its system of gavelkind inheritance, whereby land was shared equally amongst the sons. Being left with parcels of land too small to support them, men turned to crafts and trade to make a living. And with insufficient land to supply their food needs, they were obliged to buy provisions in the market place, a further stimulus.

A barber would have operated in the market – literally, because barbers were also surgeons and dentists. Bloodletting was one of their cures, along with herbal remedies. As people were illiterate, a basin served as their symbol.

If you did have toothache and went to the barber in the market place, he would offer a range of options. He might simply pull out the offending tooth with some long handled pliers. Or he might burn out the root with a red hot needle. Or, if you were afraid of surgery, he might pack the tooth with raven's dung to rot the tooth away. So you were spoilt for choice.

The entrance to The Shambles.

As mentioned, The Shambles was where the butchers and fishmongers carried out their business. The word 'shamble' simply means a butcher's market bench, from the Old English *'scamel'* or *'shamel.'*

As a butcher's bench was often a messy affair, the expression 'a shambles' came to be applied to any kind of chaotic mess. One of the best preserved shambles can be seen in York, where the butchers' hooks are still visible in the ceilings of shops beside the narrow cobbled street. The buildings in the street were arranged to keep direct sunlight off the carcasses. One can imagine a similar arrangement in Sevenoaks.

The butchers generally did their slaughtering in the street, with the blood and offal left to drain away as best it could. There was a central gutter for this purpose – such streets can still be seen in old quarters in France. Later, slaughterhouses were built, but Sevenoaks butchers were still threatened with fines for allowing blood to run into the High Street. When you consider that people dumped rubbish in the street, even sewage, and butchers were regularly told to remove large dunghills from the area, you can imagine that visiting the medieval shambles must have been an interesting olfactory experience. Unlike today, when there is actually an aromatherapist practising in The Shambles, a contrast to medieval times.

Meat was preserved by smoking or, as with the fish, salting. The butcher is salting the meat here. Salt was one of the commodities brought up the coast road, although manorial records also show that salt was carted to Otford from London.

From the turn of the 13th century documentary references to Sevenoaks market become more frequent. These usually refer to the transfer of plots or shops, but an interesting court record from 1313 tells how two men stole a heifer from Thomas Faber of Ightham, drove it to Sevenoaks, sold it in the market place and fled. So even in the early 14th century the market was being used to dispose of stolen property, something that surely wouldn't happen today.

Other trades dependent on the butchers developed in The Shambles area. There were fellmongers, who cleaned skins, curriers, who processed leather and cordwainers, who made shoes (the name deriving from Cordoba leather, but the leather used here would have been local). There were also tallow makers, who made candles or soap from animal fat, and even blood boilers, their product used for food or fertiliser. Someone once described man as 'a parasite on the cow' with some justification.

Even the horn was used to make spoons sold in the market place.

There was obviously a leather market in Sevenoaks because a 'leather searcher' was appointed to check on its quality. Just as an 'aletaster' was appointed to check on that product.

Adding to the Sevenoaks aroma, tanners were at work, using dog faeces to create the bacteria for cleaning hides. Tanning was a particularly smelly industry, although locals may not have noticed given the competition.

Of course farm produce was sold, and an important commodity was corn. Originally this would have been brought in sacks, but later it was traded by sample in the market house. A bell was rung to begin trading.

It seems that Sevenoaks, like some other Kentish markets, was a locally biased one, where locals had first choice. At Dover, for instance, trading began at 8 o'bell, when only locals were allowed to buy and sell. Outsiders had to wait for a later bell.

The old market house, re-drawn from a 19th century sketch.

A 'Market Crosse' is mentioned in a deed of 1417 and at some point this became a market house, although Ron Terry believed that the cross and the house co-existed. In 'Old Corners of Sevenoaks' he prints an enlargement from an early photograph which could show the remains of the market cross at the end of Bank Street. Confusingly, references to the 'market cross' often mean the 'market house'.

The market cross was an important meeting place, where announcements were made and deeds read aloud. The market, like the old Roman forum, was at the centre of town life.

The age of the market house, as sketched by W. Knight before its demolition in 1843, can only be guessed. It was obviously built by an archbishop because it resembles another one owned by the Archbishop of Canterbury at Maidstone.

It is a reasonable assumption that it was built in the later 15th century by the first archbishop to reside at Knole, Archbishop Bourchier, in his capacity as Lord of the Manor of Otford. Bourchier bought Knole in 1456 and did a lot of building.

The coming of the free-spending Bourchier to Knole, and the continuing success of Sevenoaks as a market town, show that by the 15th century the 'gorse-grown waste' of Sevenoaks had usurped Otford as the focal point of the manor. The thriving market and the development of Knole as an archbishop's palace were the two main factors in this.

At the market house, an octagonal timber and tile building, stalls were set up on market day in the open area underneath and the upper room was used as a corn exchange and a court house.

As well as the weekly Saturday market, two fairs were held at Sevenoaks, one on the feast of St. Peter (June 29th) and the other on the feast of St. Nicholas (December 6th). During the time of the fairs, and on market day, the local court was superseded by a special court held in the market house to sort out crimes and disputes in the fair or the market. This was the pie–powder court, run by the steward of the Lord of the Manor.

The name comes from the French *'pieds poudreux'* – dusty footed. So disputes between the dusty footed people in the market place were settled on market day in the pie-powder court.

Presumably the manorial court held here took over from the manorial court originally held at Otford (at 'The Chantry', next to the church). In Tudor times, Sevenoaks market house also hosted sessions of the assizes and the county's criminals were brought here. The town jail was nearby in the London Road at what is now 14-18, London Road (Knole House Furnishing in 2009).

A major trial held at Sevenoaks was of supporters of Sir Thomas Wyatt the younger, the son of the poet from Allington Castle. Wyatt led a rebellion against Queen Mary, fearing her proposed marriage to Philip of Spain would lead to Spanish domination. The people of Kent liked to have at least one rebellion per century (Peasants' Revolt 14th century, Cade's Rebellion 15th century).

But, despite having strong support locally, Wyatt's Rebellion was a failure and in April, 1554 he was beheaded on Tower Hill. Queen Mary then went on to endear herself to the population by burning anyone who didn't share her beliefs.

Three of Wyatt's followers, Anthony and William Knevett and a man called Mantell, were tried at Sevenoaks market house and found guilty of high treason. Despite mutterings from their supporters they were taken to the town jail in London Road prior to execution on Gallows Common.

Gallows Common was a triangle of rough land west of St. John's Hill. The placing of the scaffold varied over the centuries, at one point being close to Bat & Ball crossroads, at other times nearer the top of St. John's Hill.

Wyatt's followers were hanged here, watched by a large crowd, many of them sympathisers. The job was done swiftly to pre-empt any further unrest.

High treason was a major crime and hanging the ultimate punishment, but lesser offences were dealt with by use of the stocks, pillory or whipping post. These were usually located in the market place. Stocks are recorded in Dartford and Maidstone markets, and in Sevenoaks the stocks were at the top of the market triangle near where the fountain is today.

Here also was a cage, where offenders were locked up. And on the eastern side of the High Street, opposite the present Horncastle's, was the *'shelvingstoole'* pond, or ducking stool pond. This is where 'common scolds' were dipped. It was probably also where witches were tried. A test for witchcraft was to throw the suspect into a pond. If she floated, that proved she was a witch and she was burned. If she sank to the bottom and drowned, that proved she was innocent. So the top of the market triangle, where the two roads divide, was the place where justice was seen to be done.

A couple of hours in the stocks was a common punishment for giving short measure, selling beer without a licence, re-selling goods bought in the market or selling stinking meat or fish. You may wonder who would buy the stinking meat or fish, but nevertheless the seller would be placed in the stocks and pelted with the offending items and other rubbish. A trader who sold bad wine was forced to drink it in public. A water stealer made to walk around with a leaking bucket on his head. As far as possible, the punishment fitted the crime.

It is interesting to note that slander was taken very seriously, judging by the punishment. At Dartford, in 1545, a man found guilty of slander was forced to stand in the pillory for two whole market days, one at Dartford and one at Cranbrook. Presumably people then took the opportunity to slander him.

No doubt all these offences were condemned by the clergy, but they were not above criticism themselves. Preachers often took advantage of the large crowds on market day to put on extra sermons and whip the audience into a frenzy. Some of these had to be restrained by the Archbishop of Canterbury.

It has been mentioned that, because of the market and the growing importance of Knole, Sevenoaks outstripped Otford. It became a manor in itself in 1550.

Archbishop Bourchier at Knole was given a grant to the market in 1464, but this was not a founding charter. The main benefits to him were collecting rents from the shops and any profits from the two fairs.

In 1538, Henry VIII persuaded Archbishop Cranmer to hand over Knole, which then had a complicated history of ownership. Essentially, with Knole went the rights to the market and the fairs, and these were transferred to Baron Hunsdon (1558) and to Thomas Sackville from 1603. Apart from the times they were sold off, the rights to the market remained with the Sackvilles right down to the 20th century.

A full survey of the manor during the reign of Henry VIII says the market was held on a Saturday and was free of stallage and tollage. It says the profit from St. Nicholas Fair was seven shillings.

The way the owner of the market rights made money was through rent from the shops, tolls from outsiders at the fair ('foreigners') and charges like *'picage'*, the right to break ground for setting up a stall at the fair. Any fines were also paid to the successors of the archbishops.

In the time of Richard Sackville, the third Earl of Dorset, one record from 1612 shows he received rent from five butchers' shops in the market, two paid 20 shillings and three others one mark (13s. 4d.). Such modest perks would have been of little use to Richard Sackville, a gambler and waster, who sold the Manor of Sevenoaks and died vastly in debt.

An interesting year from later in the 17th century is 1665, the plague year. This is reflected in Sevenoaks by a 50% increase in wills and a re-making of the rental of the manor, both of which suggest a high mortality.

But Sevenoaks market survived the 1665 plague, as it had survived previous plagues and depressions.

There were 46 new market charters issued for Kent in the 13th century, usually handed out by the Crown as a favour to a magnate.

These were a potential money-making exercise, allowing a favourite to profit from tolls and rents. In fact, not all these market options were taken up, but many were and markets proliferated. However, the Black Death in the 14th century and economic depressions in the mid 15th century saw many of these artificially formed markets close.

So Sevenoaks, having sprung up naturally in a favourable position, was clearly firmly rooted. It seems the earlier a market began, the more likely it was to endure. Indeed, in 1673, shortly after the plague, Sevenoaks market was described as 'well served with corn and other provisions'. Sevenoaks market was a survivor.

As was mentioned, the large crowds attending markets were of interest to other people apart from traders. In the early 17th century Puritans put on extra sermons on market days, and in the 18th century John Wesley regularly preached in Sevenoaks.

His first open air meeting was in the old market area opposite Sevenoaks School, where he addressed what was described as 'a large, wild company'. Wesley was clearly a master of crowd control because he said that, as he spoke, 'they grew calmer and calmer until I had done, then went quietly away.' Wesley visited Sevenoaks over twenty times.

In 1774, Wesley opened a Methodist Chapel set up by one of his followers just across from the market square in what is now Redman's Lane. Eventually the Methodist church was built next to the market house in 1853, so clearly the Methodists believed in taking their message right into the market place. In the very earliest years of Christianity, under Roman rule, churches were set up in the market place. The market square, like the Roman forum, was a focal point of town life.

The market square.

As well as the market, the High Street and the market square were the setting for the Sevenoaks fairs. Eventually those two fairs, held on the feast of St. Peter, June 29th, and St. Nicholas, December 6th, were combined into one big fair held in October.

The October fair also became a hiring fair for domestic servants. They would line up in the square carrying a symbol of their occupation, hoping to get themselves employed for the following year. A servant girl would carry a mop, a cook a basting spoon. At other hiring fairs in the area, such as Wrotham, farm workers paraded in a similar way, a carter fastening whipcord to his hat, a shepherd a lock of wool. Any unhired people were mopped up at a mop fair.

A shilling usually sealed the deal and, once hired, it was illegal for workers to run away, or for anyone else to employ them. There were frequent newspaper advertisements in the late 18th and early 19th centuries offering rewards for the return of runaway employees hired at the fairs.

Sometimes they ran away because they were so badly treated – overworked, poorly fed and left to sleep in barns. Youngsters were often sent to the fair by parents who couldn't afford to keep them. If the young people ran home, the parents returned them. Hiring fairs continued well into the 20th century.

There are also records of the butter market being held in this square.

The original timber and tile market house from the 15th century was, not surprisingly, somewhat dilapidated by the early 19th century. It was considered a danger to traffic and a danger to traders so, after various attempts to patch it up, it was finally replaced by the Lord of the Manor, Earl Amherst from Knole, in 1843. It was rebuilt in stone in an attractive Regency style, with terracotta decoration added later.

The lower part was still open, to allow stalls to be set up underneath, and the upper room still used as a court house and a corn exchange. A corn market was held on Saturday afternoons, in competition with a bigger one at Dartford. Farmers to the north of Sevenoaks had to decide if they would do better at Sevenoaks or Dartford.

Competition was always a factor in market trading. Locals petitioned the Lord of the Manor in the 1750s to ask him to stop outsiders setting up stalls close to the market house 'to the very great detriment and disadvantage' of local inhabitants.

Traders in Kentish markets closer to London suffered far worse from outside competition.

At around the same time as the new market house was built, the town pond disappeared. This was the pond associated with the market for centuries, which had refreshed animals passing by or being driven to market. It was opposite No. 66, High Street (Horncastle's, 2009).

This was the *'shelvingstoole'* pond already mentioned, where those common scolds were punished. It was sometimes known as the 'cage pond', from when the lock-up was nearby. In its final appearance it had railings round it, but at one stage it was edged with willows and mallow and must have looked quaintly attractive in the High Street. By the 1840s prints no longer show it.

Its situation might seem odd in terms of water supply, but when Outram's leather shop (nearby in the reeve's house) was being restored in the 1970s, a boxed stream was found in the cellar, probably the spring which once fed the pond.

Although stalls were still set up on Saturdays, and the corn market continued to be held on Saturday afternoons, the livestock market was split off from the general one and livestock trading switched to Tuesdays. Over time, this separation of the livestock section happened with other Kentish markets.

In fact the photograph of the livestock market in the 1860s gives a good impression of how Sevenoaks market would have looked in the High Street for over 600 years, with stalls and pens filling the street right down to The Vine. On market days, through traffic would have to use London Road as the High Street became impassable. Local streets were full of animals being driven to and from the market.

People travelled some distance to trade here. Sheep were brought from Romney and cattle from Rochester. Sevenoaks market was considered very important and was described as 'one of the great markets of Kent'. So if you changed the costume according to the period, this picture gives some idea of how Sevenoaks market looked in the High Street over the centuries.

In the 19th century the October fair was still flourishing, concerned, probably as always, as much with entertainment as trade. Stalls filled the High Street, including a great many drinking booths.

There were gipsy caravans, a circus, pedlars and other travelling people, including the tooth drawer 'whose command of words and phrases was phenomenal'.

There was also Richardson's Theatre, which can be seen in the drawing to the left. The fact that John Richardson set up his travelling theatre here was a sign that Sevenoaks was an important fair, because he only attended the really big ones, like Greenwich and Southwark. He was illiterate, but died a millionaire from his travelling theatres. The shows continued into the 1850s under new management.

If you paid your money and went into the booth, in the space of half an hour you could enjoy a melodrama, a pantomime and a selection of songs. So quite a fast moving show.

In the melodramas, the plot usually involved a tussle between a rightful heir and a wrongful heir, both in love with the same young woman. After crunching plot twists, sword fights, murders, smoke, gongs and ghosts, a muffin bell rang to signal a happy ending. Better than Harold Pinter, anyway, no time for pauses.

At the colourful stalls you could buy ornaments such as busts of John Wesley, clearly a local hero. Or you might prefer a spotted cow, a French poodle, or even, surprisingly in this company, Napoleon, all done in bright biscuit china.

In the evening the stalls were lit by candles or oil lamps. One writer, the artist George Richmond, said all classes of people attended the Sevenoaks fair – the parson, the doctor, the schoolmaster – and he described it as 'the local people's fiesta'.

The impression is that, with all those drinking booths, over the years people started to enjoy themselves too much and with the growing Victorian Puritanism, many such fairs were brought to an end by the Fairs Act of 1871. Sevenoaks fair was abolished in 1874.

But some of the travelling people from the fair still continued to visit the area, including the man with the dancing bear. There are records of him visiting local villages, and even Tunbridge Wells, in the late 19th century. This form of 'entertainment' would have been familiar at the medieval fairs. It's surprising that it survived well into the 20th century when this picture was taken.

Drawing by L. Cole of the 19th century Shambles.

In the late 19th century The Shambles still had many interesting old buildings of market origin. This view is looking in from London Road, opposite South Park. Today's one remaining butcher, Williamson's, is just to the right of the drawing.

The Shambles was described as 'labyrinthine' in the 19th century, with tortuous passages. There were huts where labourers on the Knole estate lived. There was no proper drainage and, in the narrow alleys, very little light or movement of air. Water came from wells, and there are still deep wells under some present buildings in The Shambles. An interesting relic found during one conversion was a wooden rush light holder.

Butchers and fishmongers still traded here, but were gradually joined by other shops such as grocers and tailors.

The butchers used to pay the Lord of the Manor, Lord Sackville, in kind for the right of passage of animals to slaughter in The Shambles. They made an annual gift of a decorated boar's head or a festive fowl – a turkey stuffed with other birds of diminishing size.

In the High Street in the 1860s, looking south by The Chequers, it looks as though they could be cleaning up after the market. The Local Board complained it cost ten shillings a month to clean up. The road was fairly rough, just stone with gravel and clay. Local people said swallows used to gather the mud for their nests from Sevenoaks High Street.

Outside The Chequers was the regular spot for sheep pens. This was also where, on market day in the middle ages, the money changer would set up his bench (bench –'*banca*', from which we get 'bank'). The chequered board is an ancient sign for a money changer, or banker. It was also the coat of arms of the Earl of FitzWarren, who once had the power of licensing publicans.

There is a strong association of a 'Chequers Inn' with a market place because of it being the place where money was changed and accounts settled. The bench was covered in a chequered cloth. In the days when people were less numerate, this made accounting easier, with piles of coins or counters placed on the alternate squares. This is the origin of the word 'exchequer'. There was also a system using the squares for converting Roman numerals. Tokens issued by local traders, jettons, would also come into account.

If we travel south down the old Rye road, we find a Chequers Inn next to the early market (1318) at Tonbridge. At Lamberhurst, a Chequers Inn on the high street where the market was held. And at Battle, a Chequers Inn near the early market triangle.

So a 'Chequers Inn' is frequently associated with an early market place.

Towards the end of the 19th century the livestock market in the High Street was struggling. There was competition from other markets - Tonbridge, Maidstone, Rochester - but especially Tonbridge.

In 1849, Tonbridge opened a second market on the third Tuesday of the month, the same day as Sevenoaks. This is where the lack of a charter was a disadvantage because, not being a chartered market, Sevenoaks was powerless to stop the Tonbridge one. The sheep from Romney Marsh, once brought to Sevenoaks in their hundreds, were now sold at Tonbridge. Sevenoaks tried changing its day to Wednesday.

The coming of the railways in the 1860s was blamed for the further decline of Sevenoaks market in relation to Tonbridge. Tonbridge was better placed to handle stock brought by rail.

There was also antipathy towards the market from the town itself, from shopkeepers and townspeople. It was said it caused an obstruction, making people avoid the town on market day. It offended the ladies of Sevenoaks because of its smells. They were also frightened of the animals. One lady, trying on a hat in a milliner's shop, was terrified when a steer poked its head through the window. In another incident, a Sevenoaks shopkeeper was annoyed when a cow ran amok in his tobacconist's shop.

So there was growing feeling against the livestock market being held in the High Street once a month. It was suggested it should be moved or closed down altogether.

The Royal Crown Hotel, now site of The Stag theatre.

This wasn't a problem unique to Sevenoaks. Across the country, the continuance of high street markets was causing friction, and a Royal Commission on markets was set up to look into the situation.

The Royal Commission sat at the Royal Crown Hotel, London Road in July, 1888. It took evidence to try and decide the fate of the livestock market. The main objectors were shopkeepers, 16 of whom signed a petition. They said the market interfered with their business and put off their customers. Obviously the farmers and the auctioneers, Cronks, were in favour of the market continuing. The publicans, especially at The Chequers and The Blackboy, said market day was their best day for business and they would not have taken on their tenancies if it wasn't for the market.

The Rev. Jackson, on behalf of the Local Board, pointed out that the farmers made no contribution towards clearing up the mess from the market, but nevertheless the Board was in favour of the market continuing, perhaps in another location.

Probably the most crucial contributions were from Mr. Carnell, clerk to the Local Board, who said the market was established 'by ancient usage and custom' and Mr. Knocker, the Sevenoaks solicitor, who said the market had been held since 'time immemorial'.

On this basis, the market could not be legally closed. However, it continued to struggle through lack of support and faded out of its own accord in the early 1900s. The Saturday stall market continued in a reduced form.

This painting by local artist Charles Essenhigh Corke illustrates another problem for high street markets in the early 1900s. Cars were beginning to assert themselves. So now, drovers on the old droveway through Sevenoaks from Otford were coming into competition with drivers in their automobiles. This was a new problem right across the country.

Although its market use was diminishing, the market square was still a focal point and a natural gathering place at the end of the First World War, when a service of thanksgiving was held by The Chequers Inn. All the roads surrounding the market place were filled to capacity.

The Sevenoaks Branch of the National Farmers Union was formed in 1913, and one of their first decisions was to re-open the livestock market. They couldn't do this straight away, because of the war, but they acquired the rights to the market from Lord Sackville at Knole for 'a nominal sum', and by January 1918 they were ready to re-open the livestock market at a much more suitable site – on land leased from the Southern Railway Company next to Sevenoaks station.

During the negotiations with Lord Sackville, it was claimed that a medieval charter from the 1200s was found at Knole, but nothing more seems to have been heard of this potentially interesting document. There is no 'office copy' of such a charter in the Public Record Office.

The first revived livestock market at the new venue by Sevenoaks station took place on Monday, January 7th, 1918. Monday was chosen as the new market day to avoid competition, the day had varied when the market was in the High Street.

From the photograph of the sheep pens it's clear that the new market was an immediate success. The auctioneer stands on a scaffold board above the pens to take the bids. At the annual show, silver cups were presented for each section – cattle, sheep, pigs and poultry.

The Market Company which first ran it was dissolved and the auctioning taken over by Messrs. Pattullo Ltd. The Sevenoaks Fat Stock Show Association ran the Christmas show, a big and important event for many years.

So, by the station, the livestock market was flourishing once again.

The cattle pens also look full in the photograph of the Christmas Fat Stock Show in the 1930s.

The station site was well chosen. There was even a cattle dock where animals could be brought right in to the market. In the heyday of the Christmas show, cattle were sent to Sevenoaks all the way from Ireland. Once again, Sevenoaks had one of the great markets of Kent.

At the end of the 1930s the market was put to an unusual use. With the outbreak of war on Sunday, September 3rd, 1939, thousands of children from London were evacuated to Sevenoaks. They poured off the trains, and whilst their accommodation was being sorted out, they were kept in the sheep pens at Sevenoaks market. Not surprisingly, they didn't look too happy about it. Most had never been outside London before.

Many returned home when no immediate bombing occurred and came back again when the situation in London worsened.

532. High St. Sevenoaks.

Although the livestock market had disappeared from the High Street, the Saturday market lingered on. A small number of stalls continued to be set up each week on the ancient market site selling fruit, vegetables, crockery, sweets and other goods.

Some of the traders were also travelling performers in a way that would have been familiar to visitors to the old Sevenoaks fair. The cheapjack (from *'ceap'*) who sold chinaware would scatter plates concertina-wise and catch them in mid-air. The 'chocolate king' delivered a non-stop patter as he loaded bags with chocolates and toffees. The 'envelope man' brought a case full of manila envelopes, each containing something cheap but useful. And, 'before everyone's eyes', he would take out some expensive pocket watches and put them in similar envelopes and mix them with the others. The envelopes were then offered round at sixpence a time. If a customer refused one, the envelope man would tear it open and, sure enough, inside that very envelope was a pocket watch.

The Farmers Union had acquired the rights to the livestock market and the Saturday stall market was now taken over by Sevenoaks Council. Modest stall fees were charged but, interestingly, these had a local bias. In the 1920s, stallholders from the Sevenoaks urban area were charged one shilling, those from the rural area two shillings, but outsiders were charged four shillings. This local bias can be traced right back to those pannage fees from the 13th century, when the archbishop charged his local tenants twopence to pasture their pigs in the forest, and outsiders fourpence.

Another reminder of the old days of the fair. another travelling person visiting the Saturday market, was the famous Dr. Sequar.

Dr. Sequar was the travelling dentist and chiropodist. Let's hope he washed his hands between operations.

So in the early 20th century you could still get a tooth extracted in the market place, just as you could in the Middle Ages.

Dr. Sequar was famous across southern England, attending fairs and markets. He wore a top hat and tails and sold patent medicines that were guaranteed to cure all known diseases, and probably a few unknown ones.

He was accompanied by an assistant who carried a snare drum. When Dr. Sequar was extracting a tooth, the assistant would play a very loud roll on the drum to cover up the screams of the patient.

From Sevenoaks, Dr. Sequar would go down the Rye road to Tonbridge and Tunbridge Wells. At Tunbridge Wells he set up his 'shingle' on the Common. Children sang a song about him:

Good old Dr. Sequar
Good old Dr. Sequar
Give it a jerk and it doesn't hurt
Good old Dr. Sequar

Travelling dentists were banned in the 1920s, but no doubt the likes of Dr. Sequar still found some way of keeping up appearances.

The market house converted into a public lavatory.

The two main functions of the market house, the corn exchange and the court house, moved elsewhere in the later 19th century so the market house became redundant.

It was used as a public library and a technical institute. After Kent Education Authority no longer needed it, in the 1920s local councillor Tommy Skinner persuaded Sevenoaks Council to turn it into a public lavatory. It was christened 'Tommy Skinner's Palace'. The official name was still 'The Old Market House', the council acceding to the wishes of nearby traders not to have any reference to 'lavatory'. The arcaded lower part was closed in and became the 'Ladies' and 'Gentlemen's' toilets and the upper room became the caretaker's flat.

A member of the Fat Stock Association, Alan Scott, recalled that his grandparents were the caretakers and lived in the old courthouse above. He said it made an attractive flat, but unfortunately the only access to it was via a staircase inside the 'Ladies' toilet. This made him feel very conspicuous when visiting his grandparents. He would loiter outside until no-one was looking, then dash in the 'Ladies' and up the stairs.

Not everyone was happy with the new function of the market house, but the lavatories survived until the 1970s when the building was converted again for office or shop use.

In the 1950s the Saturday market consisted of a greengrocer and a few other stalls. The more colourful, if slightly dubious characters seem to have disappeared. By now cars, a novelty in that 1903 painting, had taken over the High Street with unrestricted parking on both sides.

Aerial view by Gordon Anckorn of the market by the station.

Down by the station, the livestock market was still flourishing in the 1950s and 60s. A large auction shed was built around 1960 for deadstock auctions – furniture, timber – and the sale of bedding plants and eggs.

This land had previously been the site of a sand works, with a quarry area along one edge (upper centre). At some 'junk' auctions, the items were lined up along the top of the quarry and anything that failed to sell was pushed over the edge.

In 1965, a large area next to the animal pens was surfaced over so that a new general market could be held.

The Wednesday general market began in October, 1965. There were many traders from London and Essex who did the circuit of markets – Maidstone, Tonbridge, Rye and so on. Some of them brought the colourful patter that had previously been heard at the fair or the Saturday market. There was even a 'cheapjack' juggling crockery in the traditional way and addressing the Sevenoaks crowd with lines like 'Come on, you can afford it. I've heard you've all got piles round here.'

There were stalls selling clothes, toys, cosmetics, carpets, all offering bargains, but some of the most popular sold the basic traditional items like meat, vegetables and flowers.

The butcher Malpass auctioned meat from a refrigerated lorry. There was always a throng of bidders.

The greengrocer and flower stalls were always especially popular. The Wednesday market continued at the station site for 34 years but, along with the livestock market, came to an end here in 1999 when the land was sold for development. The general market was relocated, in a much reduced form, to a car park in the centre of Sevenoaks.

It seems unfair to deal with this big and popular market in a few paragraphs but, as can be seen, in terms of the full history of Sevenoaks market, it comes very late and represents only a short blip.

Yet really, for the life and colour it brought to Sevenoaks for that time, it deserves a book to itself.

The market café, run by the Kelly family for 24 years, was at its busiest on market day, but also popular with workmen in the week and cycle clubs on Sundays.

It earned a mention in the Good Café Guide for friendliness and service.

The engraving shows market regular Ken Boustred enjoying a cup of tea *al fresco* on the balcony. Ken ate a large meal there every other day.

With the relocation, all this came to an end.

The Wednesday market continues to be held in the car park next to the bus station. The flower and vegetable stalls are still popular, but there is room for only a fraction of the stalls that used to occupy the station site. It is interesting to note that the fish van advertises fresh fish 'from Rye bay', a trade that, as we've seen, has a long history in Sevenoaks.

A stalwart of both the Wednesday and Saturday markets is Billy Westley the greengrocer. He has traded in Sevenoaks since 1983.

Johal from Essex began at the Wednesday market in 1993. He still does a weekly circuit of markets at Clacton, Sevenoaks, Rye, Ramsgate and Tonbridge, but says none of these are as busy as they once were.

The Saturday market, 2000.

At the continuing Saturday market, flowers and vegetables are popular too.

This market had its own problems when, in 1991, a Conservative government under Margaret Thatcher insisted that all council run markets should be put out to tender and given to the highest bidder. So a market that had previously been effectively self-regulating, with modest rents, was handed over to a private operator from Essex who promptly doubled the rents and caused some local stallholders to give up. Clearly the historic local bias was now a thing of the past.

There is currently a barber in The Shambles as there would have been in medieval times. His red and white striped pole, symbolising blood and bandages, a reminder of when the barber was also a dentist and surgeon carrying out bloodletting. Before becoming a barber, this shop housed the last of the fishmongers in The Shambles (Swinburne's).

The shops in this area all have large cellars, a legacy of their market origin. The Chequers in the background has that long association with the market as the place where the money changer set up and accounts were settled.

The fish stall, Saturday market.

As with the Wednesday market, there is a fish stall, in this case the fish coming from Lowestoft. It is trading, appropriately, in The Shambles area that fishmongers and butchers traditionally occupied.

As mentioned earlier, the fish trade from Rye, coming up the old drove road, played its part in the development of Chipstead and Sevenoaks markets. One of the fish traders' routes came by here in the 12th century and, today, fish is still being traded. At the Wednesday market the fish even comes from Rye, an unusual example of continuity.

The Saturday market is itself an example of continuity, having persisted in the High Street since at least the 13th century, with documentary records beginning in the 1280s. Some of the original stalls had already become shops by the 1290s. It may be small, but it is one of the oldest markets in the county.

Sadly the livestock market, which was also of ancient origin, did not survive. The following photographs record the last days of the livestock market in 1999.

Gordon Day, the chief auctioneer of Pattullo and Partners, who ran the market but didn't own the land. Gordon is auctioning sheep, standing on a scaffold board in the traditional way. The pens sparsely filled compared to the earlier picture. When Gordon began auctioning in the early 1960s there were still 400 sheep being sold on a Monday.

Les Whitear, a butcher, checking the sheep before buying. Mr. Whitear had attended the Monday livestock market since 1934 – over 60 years. Many of the butchers and farmers, like Wrotham man Paul Goodworth in the background on the right, had been coming to the market all their working lives.

In the centre is Paul Bowen from Knockholt. His family's transport firm had been carrying animals to and from the market for many years. Animals were often taken from the market directly to the slaughterhouse. There used to be one at Lamberhurst.

For centuries animals had been driven to market on foot by the drovers. The local streets would have been full of animals on market day. Even as late as the 1960s, although the practice had almost died out, people living near the market would still close their gates on Mondays to stop sheep and other animals wandering in.

Farmers claimed that the old English breeds of sheep were less trouble – it was foreign breeds like Merino that went wandering.

Butchers who had bought animals would drive them back to their own local slaughterhouses. At the top of St. John's Hill (opposite 'Avalon') was an abattoir, and people remember the cattle being driven to it up Mount Harry Road on a Monday. When the law stopped butchers doing their own slaughtering behind the shop, animals had to be transported to an approved local slaughterhouse. Slaughterhouses themselves have greatly diminished, with everything becoming more and more centralised and controlled.

Before the coming of the railway, Welsh drovers brought their black cattle across country to Surrey and Kent. Guildford market was a regular destination, but the cattle were also fattened on the Kent marshes and sold at Canterbury and Maidstone. As mentioned, sheep were driven to Sevenoaks from Romney Marsh, so animals were once driven very long distances.

Mike Gatton, a farmer from East Grinstead, was a regular at the market for over 30 years. He helped out voluntarily. Mike said the market was his 'one day of pleasure'. Like other farmers, he spent the rest of the week working in isolation but on Mondays he could meet friends and do some business.

Stan Jarvis holding the market bell. The market began with the ringing of the bell and each individual sale – sheep, cattle, hay – was also announced by the bell. Medieval markets opened and closed with the ringing of a bell, and modern stock markets begin with a bell.

Sevenoaks had a poultry market or, more accurately, a 'fur and feather' market, which attracted people from a wide area.

Caleb and John had been coming to the market for nearly forty years, dealing in chickens and rabbits. They are holding some gold lace wyandottes. Caleb said the end of the market was 'the end of life'. It was certainly the end of a way of life for many people.

Something else that was lost was a fund of expertise. Local people who kept animals could visit the market on a Monday and pick up free advice from people like this who had worked with animals all their lives.

Caleb and John were surely the sort of characters you would have seen in the market right down the centuries. As indicated, Sevenoaks is thought by most historians to be a pre-Conquest market, and if you make a careful study of the Bayeux Tapestry, you will notice this - two figures very much like Caleb and John doing some business with the local Normans.

Being a true country market, along with the rabbits they also sold ferrets, including albino ferrets which were easier to spot on a dark winter's evening.

One ferret fancier came to Sevenoaks every Monday from Thetford in Norfolk. Another said he could write a book 'Forty Years of Fun with Ferrets'. He said 'do-gooders' would put an end to ferreting, but a quick kill from a ferret was a better end for a rabbit than shooting or myxomatosis.

As well as the farmers and butchers, families went to the market to look at the animals and buy pets. Gordon Day was always being asked by London school teachers if they could bring parties of children to the market to see the animals. It was unusual to have a livestock market so close to London. Many London children had never seen farm animals close up in the flesh.

But all that came to an end in August, 1999, with the final livestock market. These are the last cattle to go through the pens.

In the background is The Farmers pub, originally The Sennocke Arms. It was here that the newly formed Sevenoaks branch of the National Farmers Union first met in 1913 and decided to re-open the ancient livestock market at the station site. Once the market got going, the pub acquired a special licence to stay open all day on Mondays to serve the farmers.

The problem for the market was that the site had become too valuable. British Rail owned most of the site and part belonged to a previous market company, Pattullo and Vinson. An area of the market which belonged to British Rail was leased but had a clause to the effect that the land could be reclaimed for development. When British Rail was privatised and became Railtrack, they wanted to sell. The other part owners also sold, so, ironically, it was market forces that spelled the end of the market.

Until recently, the only reminder of the market in this area was The Farmers pub, but even that has now gone. Re-development will leave no trace of the market.

The last Bowen lorry loading up at the last market. Some animals are more co-operative than others and the least co-operative are pigs....

As soon as you load them on, they run straight back off. Of course this is a sign of intelligence on the pigs' part because they are only going to the slaughterhouse to be turned into bacon, so they might as well make a run for it.

Even in Saxon times, when pigs were driven into the forest to feed on the acorns and beech mast, it was noted that they were difficult to control. Pigs have a mind of their own. Some of them clearly have very fine minds, because one of the attractions at the old Sevenoaks fair was 'an educated pig'. What did it do?

The very last animal to leave the last market was a kid goat. This was a sad day for the farmers, butchers, auctioneers and others for whom the market had been part of their way of life. Made even sadder by the fact that local traffic wardens took the opportunity to put lots of tickets on the cars of those who had stayed on for the final auction.

At the final auction, the auctioneer sold his own rostrum and the last item to be sold was the market bell.

Soon a different kind of animal moved in and made short work of the pens and market buildings from 1918.

It was preparing the way for redevelopment of the site with this architectural gem, described by Sevenoaks Councillors as 'brutal', 'appalling', 'an absolute monstrosity' and 'like an airport terminal.' So quite a hit.

British Telecom described it as 'BT Workstyle, Sevenoaks', but once it opened there didn't seem to be much work being done there, it always looked half empty although always fully lit. BT has already sold the building on. To rival the giant white horse at Ebbsfleet, perhaps we have a giant white elephant in Sevenoaks.

A modern office like this would be full of computers, this is how everyone works today and, ironically, after the last foot and mouth outbreak in 2001, when thousands of animals were destroyed, some farmers re-stocked via the internet.

Livestock markets continue to disappear, so perhaps this is the way of the future, markets will take place in cyberspace. Soon every aspect of life will be carried on in the shadow world of the internet. Internet shopping is already killing off high streets and general markets.

Another worry is that supermarkets will gain complete control, buying directly from farmers and dictating terms.

At the last cattle auction conducted by Gordon Day, the poster in the background had an appropriate message – 'Goodbye'.

Because in August, 1999, we saw the end of Sevenoaks livestock market. The end of that very long association with the town. The market, as we've seen, went back to the origin of the town itself, starting in a spontaneous way by St. Nicholas church, probably in the 10th century, and moving on to the High Street by Sevenoaks School before migrating to the dividing point with the London Road and occupying the High Street on Saturdays from the 13th century onwards. Today, the small Saturday market is a tiny vestige.

The livestock market, having acquired the historic market rights from the Lord of the Manor, and taken on the general market role with the Wednesday market, was the true heir to the medieval market. It was often described as 'one of the great markets of Kent' and, being pre-Conquest, was one of the oldest in the county.

But in August, 1999, we said 'goodbye' to Sevenoaks market.

MAIN SOURCES

ARTICLES:

Du Boulay F.R.H.	Denns, Droving and Danger	Archaeologia Cantiana	1961
Du Boulay F.R.H.	Late-continued Demesne Farming at Otford	Arch. Cant.	1959
Du Boulay F.R.H.	The Assembly of an Estate: Knole	Arch. Cant.	1974
Bradbury G.	Sevenoaks Market Rights (report, Sevenoaks library)		1950
Dulley A.	The Early History of the Rye Fishing Industry Sussex Archaeological Collections, 107		1969
Knocker H.W.	Sevenoaks: The Manor, Church and Market	Arch. Cant.	1926
Knocker H.W.	The Valley of Holmesdale	Arch. Cant.	1915
Mate M.	The Rise and Fall of Markets in S.E. England	Canadian Journal of History	1996
McLain B.A.	Factors in Market Establishment in Medieval England	Arch. Cant.	1997
Mitchell J.	The Public Markets of some N.W. Kent Towns	Arch. Cant	1997
West T.	As Memory Serves Me (pamphlet)		1985

Translation by Dr. N Barratt of Sevenoaks market reference in Book of Precedents by Sir Edward Coke 1614

Report of the Royal Commission, Crown Hotel, Sevenoaks, 1888

Newspapers and other papers, Sevenoaks library and C.K.S. Maidstone

Interviews with Gordon Day, Paul Bowen, farmers and other Sevenoaks people.

BOOKS:

Anckorn G.	A Sevenoaks Camera	1979
Clarke & Stoyel	Otford in Kent	1975
Dunlop Sir John	The Pleasant Town of Sevenoaks	1964
Dyson Laurie A.	The First 21 Years of the Sevenoaks Branch of the N.F.U.	1934
Everitt A.	Continuity and Colonisation	1986
Porteus G.	Dartford Country	1985
Rayner C.	Sevenoaks Past	1997
Richards F.	Old Sevenoaks	1901
Terry R.	Old Corners of Sevenoaks	2000
Ward G.	Sevenoaks Essays	1931
Watson H.	The Book of Maidstone	1981
Witney K.I.	The Jutish Forest	1976